Mother to Daughter

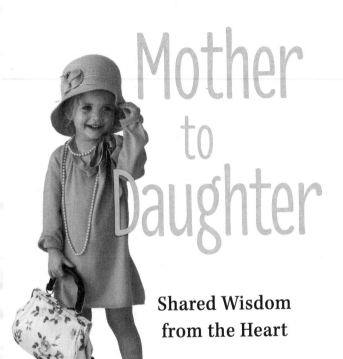

Mother to Daughter

Shared Wisdom
from the Heart

by Melissa Harrison & Harry H. Harrison Jr.

WORKMAN PUBLISHING COMPANY • NEW YORK

Library of Congress Cataloging-in-Publication Data

Harrison, Melissa, 1951-
  Mother to daughter : shared wisdom from the heart / by Melissa
Harrison and Harry H. Harrison Jr. -- Rev.ed.
     p. cm.
  ISBN 978-0-7611-7487-5 (alk. paper)
1. Mothers and daughters. 2. Parenting. 3. Motherhood. I. Harrison,
Harry H. II. Title.
  HQ755.85.S3746 2013
  649'.133--dc23

                                                        2012034401

Design by Janet Vicario

Workman books are available at special discounts when purchased
in bulk for premiums and sales promotions as well as for fund-raising
or educational use. Special editions or book excerpts can be created
to specification. For details, contact the Special Sales Director at the
address below, or send an email to specialmarkets@workman.com.

Workman Publishing Company, Inc.
225 Varick St.
New York, NY 10014-4381
workman.com
fearlessparenting.com

WORKMAN is a registered trademark of Workman Publishing Co., Inc.

Printed in the U.S.A.
First printing March 2013
10 9 8 7 6 5 4 3 2

Acknowledgments

This book was the combined effort of a number of remarkable women who shared stories of their mothers, daughters, and grandmothers. Special thanks go to Rosalie Mayo and the late Sweet Hopkins, who went above and beyond to help recruit women for this project. And the ladies in the "Bee" revealed the power of a group of women who love one another and stand by each other without even a hint of jealousy.

Gigi Berry	Sweet Hopkins	Jordan Murphy
Angela Bibb	Robbie Johnson	Susan Newberry
Judy Birkes	Sharon Johnson	Eileen Oden
Trish Bittle	Theresa Kainer	Lynn O'Shea
Steph Brinlee	Carole Kaney-Francis	Claire Parker
LaShaw Christen	Kathy King	Lisa Rees
Dena Compton	Jean Klinger	Suzanne Scott
Julianne Drost	Laurie Kohl	Christine Somers
Erika Everett	Cathy Krejci	Sara Sowan
Carol Flores	Amy Krupka	Martha Stammer
Susan Hood	Nancy McCord	Brooke Sullivan
Ivy Hopkins	Stephanie Methvin	Melissa Trycha
Kendal Hopkins	Jeannette Miesse	Tatum Tuthill

Preface

"It is a mystical relationship."
—Gigi

There have been ten jillion books about how to repair the mother-daughter relationship.

Precious few about building it.

This is what *Mother to Daughter* is about.

A mother's relationship with her daughter starts before the beginning; in fact, it starts in the mother's own childhood. Because the childhood she has determines the childhood she'll give her own daughter.

A mother teaches her daughter how to feel about herself, about handling pressure, about relishing life's joys and conquering fears. She teaches her daughter about true beauty, how to dress up, when to turn on the charm, the importance of trusting God, and how to care for a daughter of her own someday. She teaches her daughter everything she knows about being an independent woman, then gets frustrated beyond belief when her daughter acts like one.

As one mom said, "Raising a daughter is like growing a flower. You give it your best. If you've done your job well, she blooms. And after that, she leaves."

All moms instinctively know this. Maybe loving someone so much, someone who is so much a part of you, is what makes the mother-daughter relationship so special. Mothers know that love is forever. And that's a lesson their daughters can't wait to pass along.

For more parenting insights,
visit fearlessparenting.com.

The Five Keys

1. Be her mother. Not her best friend.

---

2. Let her live her own dreams. Don't try to make her live yours.

---

3. Be a strong, confident woman.

---

4. Be a good wife. You're shaping her future relationships with men.

---

5. Be aware that your goal is not to be the center of her life forever, but to work yourself out of a job.

The Bonding
Years

Get ready for the most intimate, explosive, loving relationship you'll ever have. Except for the one you had with your mom.

Start now to be the kind of mother you always wanted to be. Don't wait until she's eighteen.

Accept the fact that she is Daddy's little girl. She knows this in the cradle already.

Realize you may not
be able to imagine
leaving her and
going back to work.
That's perfectly okay.

Realize it's normal to check on her fifty times a night in the beginning.

Forget that you used to be cool and sexy. Nowadays, you won't leave the house without a stroller, a diaper bag, snacks, blankets, stuffed animals, and something to disinfect your hands.

Early on, raise her
to be adventurous.

Remember,
successfully changing a
little girl's diaper means:

1. Nothing hits you in the face.

2. Your clothes remain clean.

3. Your sense of smell
still functions.

Keep in mind that
all she wants to be
doing—for the better
part of her young life—
is what you're doing.

Know the names of her dolls and stuffed animals. Ask her to tell you stories about them.

Play tickle
monster with her.

Making her laugh will be your primary occupation. Hard-nosed investment bankers have been known to make weird faces and crazy sounds in the most public places just to be rewarded with a smile.

Be prepared.
Little girls' emotions
surprise even their
mothers.

Start off her baking career by letting her decorate the holiday cookies with sugar and sprinkles. She'll love it. She might even hit a cookie or two.

Realize that as a mom your job is to decipher if she's crying because something is wrong or if she just wants attention. Men have never figured it out.

Help her memorize
her full name and
address. This is more
important than
the ABCs.

Agree to let her brush
and style your hair.
And Dad's hair.
This urge will pass in
a couple of years.

Learn the songs she sings at school and sing them together.

Just accept that while you may have saved all your Barbie dolls for this very moment, she may play with them for . . . ten minutes.

Introduce her to the
joys of a lawn sprinkler
in the summertime.
Little girls love to
splash around.

Start saving for dance
lessons. And piano.
And gymnastics.
And swimming.
And cheerleading.
And soccer.
And basketball.
And volleyball.
For starters.

Remember,
the traditions you
establish now will
be passed on to her
daughter.

Don't feel guilty
when you absolutely
need a little space.
Just get a sitter.

Make her tea parties special events—invite all the teddy bears in the house, "eat" the cookies she hands you, pour milk and put sugar in your cup, go the whole nine yards.

Have a skipping contest. This is especially handy when you need to get somewhere fast.

Never let her question that you love her unconditionally.

Display her drawings as carefully as you display your other artwork.

Resolve not to do anything for her that she can do for herself. This will serve the two of you well for years to come.

Read to her every night—classics from your childhood, as well as her own favorites.

Watch how she talks to her dolls. You'll learn how you're talking to her.

Teach her to be a little kinder than necessary.

Enjoy the moment. Breathe. Show her that a mom can sit down on the floor and relax.

Check little brothers
and pets regularly
for glued-on sequins
and stars, glitter,
or lipstick.

Tell her she can be anything she wants. But then don't ask her why in the world she wants to be an actress or a doctor or soldier or housewife.

Put little love notes
in her lunch box.
Draw pictures if she
can't read yet.

And in the end,

Let her go.

Watch what her babysitters wear around her. Older girls are her role models.

Cherish the days when
she looks up and says,
"I love you."

Show her that even at the age of four an especially difficult day can be made better with a bubble bath.

Don't be afraid that an unhappy relationship with your mother means you'll have the same kind of relationship with your daughter. If anything, you know what mistakes to avoid.

Put on some music, crank up the volume, and show her how to boogie.

Let her fall down. Let her pick herself back up again. Let her develop determination.

Realize that
she'll know when it's
time for the training
wheels to come off.
(This will be true pretty
much her whole life.)

Don't think doing everything right will eliminate confrontations, tears, accusations, and emotional outbursts. In fact, these often mean you *are* doing everything right.

Buy her "boy" toys, too, like chemistry sets, building blocks, miniature cars, and baseball gloves.

Make dinnertime sacred.
Everyone is to attend.
Everyone will be heard.

Pop a big bowl of popcorn, sit down with her, and watch *The Princess Diaries* for the sixty-third time.

Share stories
of your mother
and grandmothers
with her.
Remember,
girls are keepers
of the flame.

Let her pick
out fabric,
then sew doll
clothes together.
If you can't sew,
help her
make paper
doll clothes.

Don't go overboard
on praise. Be specific
or it will stop meaning
anything.

Give her a garden row all her own, where she can plant sunflowers or pumpkins or cherry tomatoes. Her biggest thrill will be eating something that she grew herself.

You'll always be surprised by her stages. Even though you went through them, too.

Go on a picnic
together,
just the two of you.
Even if it's in your
backyard.

Introduce her
to the wonder and
joys of the library.
Even if you buy her an
e-reader later.

Make ice cream sundaes together. Frozen yogurt is an acceptable substitute; hot fudge is irreplaceable.

Put together a huge
box of dress-up
clothing, with different
hats and cowgirl gear
and princess "jewelry"
for her to play with.
She (and her friends)
will love this.

Teach her how
to climb a tree
(and climb back down)
and to swing across the
monkey bars. Let her
learn she's strong.

Write poems together
and preserve them.
You'll both love reading
your poetry years
from now.

She'll be hearing about
the dangers of alcohol
and drugs as soon
as school begins.
She needs to hear it
from you, too.

Take her to
the ocean.
It will be magic.

Let her smear her face
with your lipstick,
put on your earrings,
and stagger around
in your high heels.
But remind her,
no wearing makeup
out of the house until
you say so.

Teach her
manners early.
And enforce them,
even when
she's thirteen.
(Especially when
she's thirteen.)

Send her
postcards when
you're out of town.

Teach her to see the world with fresh eyes every morning.

Realize she's going
to grow up with
smartphones, laptops,
tablet computers, iPods,
and social media.
Your only hope is to
have her teach you about
these things.

Teach her to pick up
after herself.
This will serve her well
the rest of her life.

Take her to work
with you once in
a while so she can
see what you do.
(Let her help you
and she'll feel
very important.)

Keep in mind
that she's always
watching you:
how you care
for your family,
how you worship,
how you handle life.

Keep a journal
about her.
Give it to her when
she's eighteen.

Never make her
feel responsible for
your anger. Unless she
is responsible.

Praise her for
her abilities and
accomplishments,
not just her looks.

Don't think that just because school starts, your life will slow down. PTA beckons.

Remember, the secret to having deep, candid conversations with her when she's a teenager is to start having those conversations with her now.

Realize that most girls' strengths are reading and verbal communication. But introduce her to brainteasers, logic puzzles like Sudoku, and strategy games like chess, as well.

Post a rule: No whining.

When she's about seven years old, she'll start noticing what people *have*. Teach her to pay more attention to what people *are*.

Prepare her for the peer pressure she's going to face in school. It can start insanely early.

Don't buy the message that eight-year-olds should have their tummies exposed, thighs revealed, and lips glossed.

Start her skiing or snowboarding early. She'll soon be able to dust the boys.

Remember, little girls can get so obsessed with the concept of "fairness" that they'll have twenty-four-hour calculators going in their heads.

She's going to want an
iPhone when she's ten.
Give her a regular
cell phone instead,
programmed with 911,
your phone number, and
one other emergency
contact. Then lay down
laws about using it.

Buy her a diary.
With a lock and key.

Realize that one of your most important jobs is to give her a sense of self—to help her define who she is, so no one else will.

Remember to tell her she's beautiful. Inside and out.

Post her spelling
words on the
refrigerator door.
Use them in
conversation.

Make fruit-topped, Mickey Mouse–shaped pancakes together. Whipped cream and batter and fruit will go everywhere. She'll love it.

Get her
subscriptions
to her own
magazines.

Remember, when she trusts her mother to stand by her in times of crisis, she'll learn to stand up for herself.

Watch that you don't start using the word *we,* as in "we are in cheerleading" or "we are on the soccer team" or "we are in chorus." It means "we" are going nuts.

Take her shopping for pretty, special-occasion outfits. Resist the urge for matching dresses.

Take her on hikes.
Explore ponds
and meadows.
Sit outside under
the stars and point
out constellations.
Develop her love
of nature.

Teach her to write
thank-you notes.
For everything.

Make a tradition of
mothers and sisters
and grandmothers all
dressing up and going
to a fancy tea once
a year.

Help her enjoy
being a young girl.
There's plenty of time
for her to be a
young woman.

Teach her not to exaggerate.

Realize that playing
and talking with
your daughter are
more important than
cleaning house or
making dinner.

Keep in mind that eleven-year-old girls get extremely jealous. Not only of other girls, but of boys as well.

Realize that she'll gain confidence every time she does something outside her comfort zone. And succeeds.

Tell her the two of you
may disagree or even
fight sometimes.
But you will
always love her,
no matter what.

Enjoy every moment she wants to be around you. The clock is ticking.

The Awkward
Years

Realize one of life's cruelest ironies: Many girls go through puberty at about the same time their moms enter menopause.

Be prepared. The sweetest, gentlest fifth graders have been known to metamorphose into sullen, angry, mean creatures who want nothing to do with their families.

Assure her it's okay
that she's eight inches
taller than the boys.
They'll catch up.

Just accept that one moment she'll be clingy, and the next moment she'll be pushing you away.

Now you have someone to enjoy chick flicks with. Leave grumbling Dad at home.

Encourage her to
spend time with
her grandmother.
For some strange reason,
they'll get along fine.

Teach her that perfume shouldn't knock a family out of their chairs at breakfast.

Start a mother-daughter
book club with other
moms and daughters.
Take turns picking
books—remember,
you have to read what
she chooses, too.

Give her a little rope.
Let her learn from her
mistakes while the
stakes aren't so high.

Accept that by the time she's in middle school she doesn't want you to know every thought in her head. And really, you don't want to know, either.

Help her identify her strengths. And help her strengthen her weaknesses.

Realize that everything in middle school is competition—friends, popularity, grades, clothes. She's under a lot of pressure.

Enforce three rules early on: No eye rolling. No door slamming. Mutual respect.

Remind her to respect her teachers. They hold the key to a lot of awards, honors, and recommendations.

Spend your one-on-one time doing not just what interests you, but also what interests her.

Understand that for girls, independence usually starts with hair. Ask yourself, how important is it, really, if it's blue?

You'll have moments when you feel like mom of the year. And moments when you're convinced you've failed her. In the same conversation.

Make sure she and Dad spend time together. They both need each other.

Don't feel guilty about being the nosy mom who always checks to see if other adults are at home at her friends' houses. It'll keep her out of trouble.

Tell her how well
she's doing.

Remind her that neither one of you is always right. But you're always the mom.

Have a girls' night
with her once a
month—a night when
you paint toenails,
watch silly TV shows,
laugh, and have fun.

You'll worry about her not belonging. Ultimately, despite all your best help and support and advice, it's beyond your control.

Remind her that bullying is a serious issue, and teach her when she should stand up for herself and when to tell an adult.

Teach her that the last reason not to try something is the fear she may not do it well.

Ask her what color she'd like to paint her bedroom. Then spend the weekend painting it with her.

Don't let her moods dominate the house. Or else it will be one insane house.

Don't wait for her grades to slip before you become the homework police. Review her homework nightly.

Keep in mind that a lot of girls today have *too much* going on outside school.

By middle school you
can tell what kind
of brains God gave
your daughter.
And if she's using them.

Encourage her
to do a little good
every day.

Keep in mind,
even Mother Teresa
would be driven nuts
by a middle-school-age
daughter.

If she temporarily
loses her spine,
help her find
it again.

Adolescent girls
can be cruel.
Be there for her
when her feelings
get hurt.

Volunteer at her school—chaperone a dance, paint scenery for a play, shelve books in the library. It's a great way to participate in your daughter's life.

Don't panic if she
wants to wear thong
underwear at thirteen.
That's all she's ever
seen advertised.

Let her have some control over the car radio, even if it hurts your ears. Try not to comment on her music. Really, really try.

Many former tomboys
end up with
"girlie" daughters,
and vice versa.
That's just how it goes.

Respect her wish
for privacy.
Explain to her father
why his daughter
needs to spend
ninety-seven hours
holed up in her room.

Remember,
in even the healthiest
mother-daughter
relationships,
rebellion sets in.
Hug her, pray for her,
wait for her to
come back.

Remind her that girls who act dumb to attract boys attract dumb boys.

Remember,
if a TV or computer
or smartphone isn't
in her bedroom,
she'll find it easier
to study—and sleep.

There are advantages
to playing chauffeur:
Teenage girlfriends
talk nonstop in
the backseat.
About everything.

When words
utterly fail, small,
kind gestures like a
note or text or a funny
card remind her that
Mom really cares.

Remember,
a cell phone is
a lifeline when you
start dropping her
off at the mall or
a concert or a game.

Point out to her that truly smart girls listen more than they talk. But they also know when to speak up.

Don't carry grudges.
You're teaching her
to do the same.

Never make the
mistake of thinking
if you do just a little
more for her,
she'll magically
become happy.

Teach her the art
of disagreeing without
being disagreeable.
It will take her far
in life.

Understand that you can't know enough about her at this age: where she's going, who she's going with, what they're doing, who they're meeting, when they'll be home.

Discipline with what's important to her. Take away her computer and cell phone and you've removed access to her social life. Place a temporary ban on soccer or her friends' parties. Seems harsh, but all's fair in love and raising daughters.

Remember,
how much she tells you
is all about how you react.
If you go ballistic and
throw a tantrum over
every little thing,
she'll clam up.

Remind her that the cookie-cutter seventh and eighth graders on TV shows don't really exist.

Keep hugging her.

Participate together in a fund-raising walk for breast cancer research. Let her discover the power of thousands of women coming together for a cause.

Don't ever let
her believe that
"Whatever" is a
conversation.

Don't forget,
you are as big a
mystery to her as
she is to you.

A lot of girls find it
safer to take their
frustrations out on
their mothers.
Tell her, ever so sweetly,
that you will have
none of this.

Show her how
to walk in heels
without tumbling
over.

Take pictures even
if she whines,
"Mom, don't!" Later,
she'll be glad you did.

Insist she take part in family traditions. Happily.

Enforce your rules, keep your standards high, but keep telling her you love her.

Remember,
she needs a minimum
of eight hours of sleep.
Impose a bedtime
curfew.

Try to go for a day without criticizing or correcting her.

Get her involved
in volunteer work
in your community.
The trick is to take
her mind off herself.

Accept that
everything you do is
going to embarrass
your daughter.
Especially being
a good parent.

Every now and then,
hold her hands,
look her in the eye,
and tell her she's
the daughter
you always wanted.

Girls & Beauty

To some parents,
makeup is ChapStick;
to others, it's lipstick
and nail polish.
You're the mom here.

Explain to her dad that most girls start getting their ears pierced around the age of ten. (He'll think twenty is more appropriate.)

Let her know she doesn't need makeup and highlighted hair to be beautiful.

Allow her to wear what she feels great in. If there's nothing scandalous about it, let it go—even if it's not your style.

Show her pictures
of yourself when you
had geeky glasses,
bad hair, and horribly
lame clothes.
By her standards,
anyway.

If her father ever says she's fat, whack him.

Give her the confidence to wear what she wants despite the dictates of fashion.

Encourage her to compliment other girls on their clothes.
With sincerity.

If she doesn't see a problem with the length of her skirts or shorts, suggest she model them in front of her father.

Clue her in to the airbrushing techniques, plastic surgery, and makeup artists that enhance the "naturally" beautiful celebrities and models she sees in magazines.

Teach her that no shoe
in the world should
require a woman to
have foot surgery
to wear it.

Show her how to dress like a million bucks with clothes from the sale rack. There will come a day when this is a life skill.

Teach her that the real secrets to fashion are posture and poise, voice and speech, etiquette and style. And these secrets can be learned.

If her skin is
a problem,
don't hesitate
to get her to
a dermatologist.

Realize that no matter what your daughter wears, your husband will look at you and ask, "Do you think it's okay if she wears that?"

Be prepared:
She will compare
her clothes to the
other girls'. She will
want to blend in,
not stand out.

Don't forget, her skin
might break out,
she might have to
wear thick glasses,
her hair might do weird
things—but she still
needs to think of herself
as a beautiful person.

Make sure she understands never even to *experiment* with shoplifting. The number of girls who think they can get away with it is just staggering.

Teach her that one of the secrets of beautiful women is a good dentist. Straight, healthy, white teeth can turn more heads than cosmetic surgery.

To truly understand
the generation gap,
visit one of
"her" stores.
Moms have been
known to experience
hallucinations in
these places.

Realize she'll be horrified if you try to buy anything from one of "her" stores.

By eighth grade,
the highest form of
entertainment for her
and her friends will be
going to the shopping
mall by themselves.
Impose credit card limits.

When she starts shopping without you, remind her that Mom reserves the final right of approval. Be ready to return a lot of stuff.

Accept that your daughter may be a born fashionista who has a better sense of style than you.

Stress the importance of being fit over being thin. A lot of impressionable girls are totally confused about this.

Remember,
the importance she
attaches to labels is
directly proportionate
to who's paying.

Explain that real beauty isn't about a skinny body or shiny hair. Being beautiful on the inside is what really matters.

When she tells you that your hairstyle is wrong, your shoes are lame, and your jeans have got to go, it means she's trying to help you look sixteen. Resist.

Tell her it's okay
to sometimes kick
off her shoes and
walk barefoot.
Even in a prom dress.

Girls &
Other Girls

Remember,
everything she learns
about trusting women
starts with you.

Teach her early on not to let other girls define who she is.

Remind her that
if she makes fun
of her friends,
she's setting herself
up for a lonely life.

Encourage her to
make friends at school,
on sports teams,
at church, in the
neighborhood . . .
to have a wide range
of friends from
different backgrounds.

Remember,
one of the hardest
things for a mom to
watch is when her
daughter is on the outs
with her friends.

Explain to her that
for a while, mean girls
will be popular.
But the mean girl
should never be her.

If she's being
ostracized,
make a lot of time
for her on weekends
and evenings.

Explain to her father
that hiring a hit man to
take care of the mean
girls isn't an option.

Teach her that
the girl who says,
"If you talk to *her*,
I won't be your friend,"
will never be a
true friend.

Tell her about your high school reunion. That some of the happiest, most successful former classmates were basically unknowns in high school.

Teach her that a friend
is somebody she can
share her greatest
successes with and who
will be honestly happy
for her.

Remind her that beauty, money, or popularity doesn't protect against meanness. But kindness can overcome it.

There are mean girls and then there are bullies. Teach her to know the difference, and encourage her to seek your guidance if she's being truly harassed.

Make your house the hangout house—filled with snacks and drinks and movies, where her friends are always welcome.

Teach her how to connect with other women and you've given her one of life's great gifts.

Remember,
she may not want
to talk to you, but her
friends often will.
Ask away.

Teach her that the really, really kind person is never forgotten.

Girls & Boys

Tell her why you decided to marry her father. Then tell her the rest of the story.

Start discussions about
your expectations,
morals, and values early.
If you wait till
eighth grade,
you've waited too long.

Keep in mind, there are actually *two* major talks you'll have with your daughter. Before the "Boy Talk," there's the "What's Happening to Your Body Talk."

She may bring up the
"Boy Talk" anywhere.
Like driving home
from volleyball.
Don't flinch.

Learn her lingo. "Dating" a boy in middle school might mean she talks to him in science class.

Understand
she has to get
the facts from you.
Girlfriends are
just chock-full of
misinformation.

Be aware that music, TV, magazines, movies, and the Internet promote a hypersexual lifestyle. Make sure her values are not their values.

Remember,
boys magically
show up at girls'
slumber parties.
Plan accordingly.

Keep in mind that only a fourteen-year-old girl could find anything remotely attractive about a fourteen-year-old boy.

Make sure she knows she can tell you anything. The fewer secrets at this age, the better.

Point out that if she wears clothes to draw boys' attention to her chest, attention will be drawn. Then what?

Don't stay up late worrying that your daughter doesn't have a boyfriend. Get a life.

Teach her that
no man is worth
betraying another
woman for.

Remember,
even if she's made
a decision to delay
sex, you need to keep
talking to her about it.

Be careful about judging a boy by his looks. Learn something about him first.

Teach her how to *expect* to be treated by a man. So she'll know when she's not being treated well and will refuse to tolerate it.

Tell her to find a boy
who won't think a date
to worship services
is weird.

Warn her about the dangers of online "relationships." She should know never to give out real information or take anything at face value.

Don't push her into a relationship just so she can be popular.

Remind her and her
dates that she must
be home on time,
bright-eyed and happy.
Or else.

Don't fall "in love"
with any of
her boyfriends.
They will come and go.

Encourage her
to invite her
boyfriends over
for dinner.

Encourage her
not to thwart
chivalry when she
encounters it.

Tell her she needs to decide where her limits are before she finds herself in the heat of the moment. Because then there are no limits.

Explain that men will always feel they need to offer her advice. It's not their fault. They're genetically wired that way.

Stay out of her love life. Never give a strange boy your daughter's phone number.

Remind her that reputations are fragile. And they follow you around.

Keep Dad involved.
Don't hesitate to bring
him in when the issues
get more serious.

When a boy breaks
her heart, curiously,
you'll find yours
in pieces, too.

Girls &
Extracurricular
Activities

Develop her interest in sports early. Even if you never played anything. It will influence her physical, mental, and moral well-being for the rest of her life.

Remember,
everything is more
competitive than when
you were her age.
Everything.

Encourage her to try a lot of different activities. But don't invest a ton of money in any of them until she's ready to make a commitment.

Practice soccer or basketball or softball with her. Even if you're terrible at it.

Here's the deal about private lessons:

1. They cost a fortune.

2. Other girls are getting them.

3. Your daughter may quit in three years anyway.

Don't confuse your
dreams with hers.
Maybe she doesn't
want to be
a cheerleader.

Coach her team if you
know the game.
Cheer on the sidelines
if you don't.

Be a soccer mom. It's a great life.

Remember, adolescent girls are defined by their activities: "She's in choir, she's a gymnast, she's an equestrian."

If you take her defeats harder than she does, you're not helping things.

Remember,
she just may be
a large girl.
If she's physically fit,
who cares?

Try not to sugarcoat
a difficult loss.
High school girls
take losing hard.
And the better
the athlete,
the harder the loss.

Explain to her that
Dad may suddenly be
overcome by this urge
to paint his stomach,
his car, his face with
her team colors.
This is how men think.

Be calm about all her tryouts. She can't worry about you *and* her performance.

Keep in mind
that tryouts for
anything can be
hard on mothers and
daughters. And fathers.
Even brothers.

Don't give her a
speech when she loses.
Give her a hug and
a pizza.

It's normal to lie awake at
1 a.m. after she decides
not to try out for the
cheerleading squad despite
ten years of private dance
and gymnastics lessons
and wonder,
"What did we pay for?"
You kept her active, graceful,
and in good health.

Remember,
this is all
extracurricular.
Grades come first.

Realize that competitive girls' sports are cutthroat, vicious, expensive, sometimes bloody, and often humbling. Just like life.

Make sure her
coaches know
what they're doing.
Then leave them alone.

Teach her to
win honorably.
And to lose
with grace.

Girls & Money

In spite of what
she tells you,
all she really needs
is food and clothing
and shelter and love.
The rest is gravy.

Teach her how to budget her spending. Even if her only source of income is babysitting.

Remind her she's
been blessed by God.
And she must give
something back.

Explain that if she ever loans money to a friend, she could wind up losing both.

Challenge her to figure out tips in restaurants and sales tax and percentage reductions in stores to hone her math and money skills.

Show her how to
negotiate . . . for a car,
a raise, a discount,
a home.

Encourage her to find
a summer job that
matches her interests,
whether it's working at an
animal shelter, day camp,
or clothing store.
She'll earn money
and real experience.

Review with her the
costs of college and the
impact of scholarships
and financial aid
in light of your
family's own financial
situation.

Because student debt is a serious responsibility, encourage her to make thoughtful choices when it comes to choosing a college and a major.

Teach her to always carry a zero balance on all her credit cards.

Give her money smarts.
Explain how to balance
a checkbook,
the dangers of spending
more than you make,
the importance of saving.

If she says all her friends are carrying $450 purses and she wants one too, smile, hug her, and suggest that she find a job.

Remind her to spend less than she could. And to give back more than she should.

Help her invest in a
mutual fund when
she's in high school.
She's never too young
to start financial
planning.

Teach her never to be afraid to face and deal with financial fears.

Girls & Success

Remember,
girls whose parents
have high expectations
for them also have
high expectations for
themselves. It just
works out that way.

Work with her
on her study skills.
How else will
she learn?

Help her understand
what it means
to be successful.
You and your daughter
should both know
the answer . . .
in detail.

Keep in mind that
you can only provide
her with opportunity.
The rest is up to her.

Remind her that the path to success often requires a mentor.

Never let her forget
that the only thing she
can control in this life
is her mind.

Help her learn the art of conversation. It will take her everywhere in life.

Talk to her about first impressions—ones she's formed about other people, and the impressions people will have about her.

Never take credit for her successes. Or the blame for her failures.

Give her responsibility before she reaches adulthood. She'll make mistakes, of course, but there will also be times when she'll really impress you.

Teach her that
enthusiasm is
one of life's
greatest gifts . . .
and that it can
be learned.

Let her know she can be successful while still being kind and considerate.

Remind her that some of the most successful people in the world just had to deal with setbacks because self-indulgence was an option they could not afford.

Teach her that the healthiest women are the ones who are independent.

There will be times
when she says life
is unfair. Explain to her
it was never a given
that life is fair.

Show her how to ask
for what she wants.
Then to accept the
outcome.

Inevitably, games
will be lost, student
council elections will
go the wrong way.
Don't encourage her to
quit when the going gets
hard. Encourage her to
develop some muscle.

Tell her it's
the end result
that matters.
Not where
you start.

When she's older,
remind her that young
girls now look up to
her as a role model.

Never forget, the greatest barrier to her success could be too much criticism from you.

Teach her that willingness to accept responsibility for one's own life is what separates the women from the girls.

Girls &
Spirituality

Tell her that
God created her
as an answer to
your prayers.

Encourage her to make choices wisely. Because even the smallest decisions can have the biggest consequences.

Teach her to find ten blessings a day. Twenty on bad days.

Stress God early in her life. Don't wait until she's in high school and in trouble to insist she go to church or synagogue every week.

Teach her to talk to God throughout the day, when things get rough *and* when things go well.

Never forget that
you can't teach your
daughter about God
if you don't have a
relationship with Him.

Remember,
teaching her about
God is not unlike
teaching her about sex.
It's not done all at
once—it's the way you
live your life every day.

Share your
most mystical
experience
with her.
Over and over
again.

Don't let her turn her back on life's blessings. Teach her to stay the course.

Teach her that
God gives us all
different gifts.
It's how we use
them that matters.

Let her see you give
of yourself unselfishly.
Not just your money,
but your time,
your patience,
and your love.

Encourage her to pray
for the people she
doesn't get along with.
One day it could
be you.

Fill your house with warmth, love, and joy, and you'll find it's also filled with her and her friends.

Tell her that
some of life's most
puzzling questions
have no simple
answers.

You will have to remind her that God has a plan. And maybe it's not for her to be a Tri-Delt, but something even more special.

Older Girls

You might easily
prefer her boyfriends
to her girl friends.
Be prepared.

Smother her with love. Not advice.

Don't give her rope
to mope around
the house. Get her up
and push her out into
the world.

Keep your chin up. Your real daughter will come back.

Teach her to
respond to insults
with class.

Discuss the non-negotiables about driving: the seat belt, the speed limit, zero texting, zero alcohol and, if she's driving your car, no fast-food wrappers or other trash left in it.

Show her how to fill a gas tank without getting gas on her stilettos.

When necessary,
remind her that
reckless adolescent
behavior will lead to
a permanently
parked car.

Teach her never to get into a car with a drunk girl or boy at the wheel. That she can always call you to pick her up, no questions asked.

Realize that some girls don't know when they're being drama queens and when they're truly distraught.
But wise moms do.

Remember, there may come a time when she won't understand why she can't stay out till 2 a.m., date a bad boy, study only one hour per week, or live apart from the family.

Do not fall into the "I just want her to be happy" trap. Happiness for her is probably foregoing homework and driving a Beemer at sixteen.

Introduce your daughter to a gynecologist by the time she turns fifteen. Tell her she's free to find her own as long as she keeps regular appointments.

Instead of starting World War III over her room, just tell her she can't have any new clothes until she picks up what she already owns for three months straight.

Teach her how to change a tire, to use an electric drill, to mow the lawn. She should never have to depend on some guy to do these things for her.

Join a gym together.
You could probably
use the exercise,
and she could use the
one-on-one time.

Those problems she's telling you about? The best way to help her is to just listen.

Use the things she tells you in confidence against her and you've committed the ultimate betrayal.

Challenge her to take the honors and advanced placement classes her school offers. Coasting along may cost her the college of her choice.

On the other hand, she may be smart enough to handle five AP courses, but she may not have the time or strength. Help her to understand her limits.

A daughter who
grows up with love
and discipline will
anticipate her mother's
reactions to the
choices she makes.

Remind her that if she doesn't feel good about herself, no one around her is going to feel good about her, either.

Teach her how to recognize dangerous situations. If she feels her heart racing, it's time to get out of there.

Give her options she
can use to get out
of bad situations.
Review them regularly.

As difficult
as it may be,
accept her
apologies.
With affection.

Recognize that for all her pulling away and moods and arguments, there will be times when she wants nothing more than to talk to her mother.

Sometimes,
all you can do
is be there.
Without words.

Give her a budget
for her prom dresses
and shoes and dinners
and limos and
after-parties.
Make it lower than
your house payment.

Realize that if you still want to be involved in every aspect of her life, you really don't have enough to do.

Tell her it's a good idea to make friends with people smarter than she is.

Remember, a time will come when you will say, "*You* figure it out." It will be hard on both of you.

Encourage her
to travel.

Give her the great books you want her to read someday.

Caution her about hanging around people who like to just "kill time." That phrase says it all.

Tell her to be careful about who she reveals her personal life to.

Take heart in knowing you might actually talk to her more often on the phone when she's away at college than you did when she lived under your roof.

Tell her if at first she doesn't succeed, do it the way Mom would have told her to do it in the first place.

Encourage her to
settle her arguments
in minutes.
Not to hang on to
them for weeks.

If she's trying to choose between a boyfriend and a scholarship, insist she take the scholarship.

Tell her not to worry about being better than a man. Just be better as a woman.

Remind her that life is nothing if not a daring adventure.